Wildflowers

K.J. Bashford

i

Dedicated to all the wildflowers who live amongst the weeds but continue to outgrow all that is around them.

CONTENTS

Roots..........3

Weeds..........59

Leaves..........120

Wildflowers.........163

You have wondered into my garden.

Each one of these poems act as a single wildflower.

Please take care of each of these flowers as they are all are special in their own way.

To all of the little wildflowers who feel like they don't belong, your individuality is what

makes you outshine the rest of the garden.

I hope that you know you are cherished and remember how special you are.

Thank you.

-K.J. Bashford

Be a wildflower

an individual

a believer

someone who stands out from the crowd

a soul that shines brighter than the sun

ROOTS

Wildflowers

My mind is like the ocean

thoughts roll in slowly

sometimes they crash into each other

I think about the many things that float along in my head

when high tide comes, it's hard to think clear

the storms can be choppy too

my thoughts become twisted and nasty

if the water is calm, my mind is clear

my thoughts stay happy and I am less weary

I may seem so unpredictable when everything collides

I just gently float along not knowing where I'll end up next

K.J. Bashford

Our relationship taught me a lot about what love really is and

that it never really existed between us

Wildflowers

I was the broken toy that nobody wanted

you came along and tried to fix me

by doing so,

 you only damaged me more

K.J. Bashford

Loving you was a risk

Strangers

lovers

strangers again

K.J. Bashford

Our conversations never had any substance

Wildflowers

I trusted you too easily

you never trusted me at all

K.J. Bashford

You hurt me just as fast as you fell in love with her

I was a happy care-free kind of girl

I danced among the wildflowers

moved to the sound of life

until I met you

then everything about me changed

We were just friends, nothing more

"I am okay with that." you said

"I'll have to be okay with that." I said

What am I to you?

a few months flew by and we were so happy

it was just the two of us

we painted the sky with colors of joy and love

then all of the sudden our worlds began to separate

 a storm was created

it felt like it would never end

moments of silence made the days drain by

lightning struck my heart as thunder rolled by

you started to move on from me, not a care in the world

were you ever going to speak me again?

it is me putting in all the effort even after you said we were

     okay

who am I to blame?

     myself.

yes. sure, that's what it is

it must be because I can't seem to keep you close

my heart, it burns and my soul aches

you don't want me

I know it is over

I'm trying so hard now

what's the point?

please come back to me, I love you so

I don't want you to go but if that is a must I need to know

I am here, I am all yours

I do not want to wear your heart on my sleeve if you want it
elsewhere

please tell me so

again, I ask, what am I to you?

Wildflowers

Our love was always meant to be temporary

K.J. Bashford

He wanted you to be what could never exist

Wildflowers

Please listen to me

all the things you've done were not wrong

 you don't need him

he doesn't really want you as you are

take your heart with you and never let him break it

K.J. Bashford

We only hate what we don't have

Wildflowers

Some days I have bad moments

your energy sits heavy upon my shoulders

you climb into my head and twist my thoughts around

I want to be okay

I am getting better but I never know when these little

        moments will hit

when they do, I don't know how to handle myself

K.J. Bashford

Sometimes darkness spreads over the light

it lays itself down like a heavy blanket

suffocating whatever lies beneath it

it could be scary when we do not see it coming

darkness seeps through the cracks in the walls

looking to take the light away

it sits upon our shoulders

weighing us down

we can't do anything

it suppresses us into depression

wrapping around our souls

taking us down into nothing

My heart aches so much, yet I still have so much love for

you

Thinking about the idea of you makes me sick

Wildflowers

My body felt like a piece of rotten fruit

it was bitter sweet like a peach

I kept trying to put people back into my life who weren't good

for me

Wildflowers

I want all of these uneasy feelings to escape my body

I feel like I am in shackles with problems bound all over me

I want to leave, move on from this past

I keep moving forward but YOU keep pushing me back

A rock sits at the bottom of my stomach and completely

    weighs me down

I can't accept that you are with this girl

but knowing that what you did to me you will unravel onto her

leaving you, once again

    alone

Wildflowers

We try so hard to undo our past,

but the past is what unravels our future

K.J. Bashford

What happened to forever?

Wildflowers

I know you are hurt

 I know we need time

Please show me that deep down somewhere, you are still

here

K.J. Bashford

You are so unoriginal

it's disgusting

Wildflowers

Anxiety sits heavy on my shoulders

it runs through my veins, claws at my eyes

I try to peel it off my skin but each time it comes back

        stronger and thicker

some days are better than others

but it circles my mind from time to time

I can't do certain things or talk to people

anxiety does it to me, but yet I get blamed for it

K.J. Bashford

I got really good at pretending because of you

Why did you pick me to hurt?

You both had one thing in common:

me

Wildflowers

I hoped that someday you'd want to come back to me

    to unravel the truth

you were so naive

you only came back wanting to fuck me instead

K.J. Bashford

I'm not the first person you think about anymore

you don't call me if you need me

knowing that I can't be there for you brings me so much pain

it's different now that you have her

Wildflowers

Why did you continue to kiss me when your lips had

already been elsewhere?

K.J. Bashford

I constantly made excuses for you

Wildflowers

It grows like weeds

spreading like a damn disease

dropping on my body thinking it will please me, satisfy me

but this whole time I can't fucking breathe

my skin is crawling with you all over it

K.J. Bashford

A night of passion was all it took

two lovers pressed together, completely hooked

the smell of liquor stung the air

smoke clouded up each corner of the room

clothing stripped off, one piece at a time

he caressed you softly as you looked at him with your weary

      blue eyes

he pressed into you with all his might

a release came

 it shuttered in your body, you wanted to put up a fight

chills ran up and down your spine

feeling weary and uncertain you cried for help

he was there

you grumbled and moaned at his quick movements

he made you feel good but it didn't last

sweet bitterness took a bite out of your heart

you say you love him, but does he love you?

another night rolled by, nestled under the sheets once again

a moment of lust, bodies entangled despite the mistrust

he became fuzzy in your mind, as you looked into his eyes

you think "is this real?"

he wrapped up his work and is pleased at his sight

you felt you made love to him but was it even right?

morning swept in, you both lay close

the sun peaked through the blinds signaling that it was time

     to get up

you wrapped the sheets around your body as you

     shuffled into the bathroom

he followed behind, as he flicked the dim light on

you knew that it was time but were too scared to look

you sat down in the bathroom, body stiff and shaken up

he reminded you that it needs to be done

"be patient" you say as this was not fun

the reading is here and it is clear

you look down in your hand and there it appears

two tiny pink lines pop up at the same time

your first reaction was to throw your head back and laugh but

instead your heart sank

you placed your hands down onto lap

he looked at you, knowing it was true

he held you close as you leaned into him for comfort

it was not long until he said that he loved you but it must go

a disregard to your choices and feelings but you knew it was the
        best thing to do

no future planned out, no money had been saved

it was inevitable, but a hard problem to face

two months along and you didn't know

the things you did and choices you made

they were wrong and hurtful, maybe effecting not one but two
        heartbeats, causing a mistake

this is not your fault

you did not know, but you did the right thing to get results

it is okay, this is what is best

you had time to think but the decision was made

his words rested in your head making them impossible to
        fade

in the waiting room, you sat, legged crossed, with your hands
        on your knees

your name was called, the nurse comes out

in the room, you sat, dressed in a gown

the doctor comes in and tells you its time

he laid down the rules and explained what he had in mind

he gave you the option, choice in hand

you have the right, it is your body

he placed a hand on your arm, and kindly smiled

you look down at yourself not shedding a tear

inside you are crying but are too scared to let go

sadness filled the room as you prepared to say goodbye

you felt so alone as you parted your ways

but you knew you'd be okay because someday you'd meet

    again

K.J. Bashford

There was never anything

yet, I felt that we were everything

Wildflowers

The hardest thing I had to do was leave you

K.J. Bashford

It's sad knowing that what you did to me you'll do to her

I hope she realizes that you don't deserve her

K.J. Bashford

Placed in a crowded room

low-lighting and blaring music filled the space

 bodies pressed up on one another breathing in the sweat

    and alcohol

 I hung back and watched as intoxication took over

drugs lurked around the corner, broken bottles scattered the

    floor

my sneakers sat soggy in something sticky

my head spun with everything going on

boys grabbed the girls who didn't want to be touched

the girl's best friend held her hair back while she threw up

    but she kept taking shots to numb her pain

 smoke made it unsettling in the room

I thought in that moment everything would turn cold and blue

it was then I realized I was face-to-face with a temporary

    reality

Wildflowers

We are so caught up in planning our future

we end up dwelling on the past

forgetting to live in the present

Stillness wrapped around our bodies as we stood in the room
> facing each other

I walked towards you and sank down onto the bed

tears slid down my red cheeks as I looked into your weary
> eyes

you were prepared to fight

flames burned in your chest as you sat there ready to listen

I poured my heart out onto yours

sharing how I felt, and how I wanted more

our differences are what you felt pulled us apart

we came from two separate worlds that could never mix

I cried to you asking please don't go

you said it was not over, just not the right time

my heart raced as my teardrops dripped down onto your
> skin

you picked up my hand, ran your fingers through it

I knew in that moment we were okay

everything felt good, we were happy again

you kissed me softly, pressing into my body

you looked at me as you removed my clothing piece by piece

it was then I knew you made love to me for the first time

stars danced across the room

the whole galaxy wrapped around us

I knew then I loved you

I loved you even before but wanted to wait

a month ago, you said it was too soon say

now we both felt what we have been yearning for, for so

      long

I asked if you wanted me to stay, since we just sort of just

      parted ways

you popped up your head and said "sure"

you asked for my phone to play some music

we ordered a pizza and spoke just a bit

you suddenly felt distant and I knew what I did

I tried to follow you around the room

but you were too quick and escaped too soon

I watched you as you began to slip through my fingers

I knew this was the end of something beautiful

I gathering my things, and all that I gave you

I said, "I think I'll go now"

"Yes, why don't you", was your reply

sorrow sank deep down into your eyes

you got up and yelled, words ripped through your voice

you saw what I did, looked through my phone

I did the unthinkable, I felt so shallow

I broke our trust and mixed it with lust

my mind was a blur and I wanted more

he carved at my broken body until it was hollow and he was
>satisfied

but I hurt the person I love most because my enemy found a way

that lured me back once more

his words twisted my mind, faded out reality

I couldn't tell what was wrong or right

the whole time I was there with him, I knew my heart belonged
>to you

you asked why I did it and I said it wasn't for me

it was not fun,

it was really scary

but getting away from my monsters is something that's not
>easy

he was forceful, put me down and manipulated me

I wanted to run, run into your arms

you were my support, my world and my love

I did what I did, and yes it wrong but I want you know that it wasn't
the girl you fell in love with

I hope that you can see me for who I am and not who he
made me

the abuse strains my body

it weighs me down, the shackles hit hard as I reach out for
you

I became broken once again because it was all that I knew

I tried to get away but if I said no only worst things would
come

I was scared and defeated but I knew that if I told you, you
would understand

you know me for me,

I know you see that happy, care-free girl that shines from my
soul

but deep down her body is brittle and her bones are ridden
with anxiety

I know you are hurt, I know you hold anger

but I want you to know that my heart belongs to you

I hope you can understand and hear my plea

I come from an abusive standpoint you see

it is never easy

  I am getting stronger but some days are getting harder than

      others

let's work this out, let me hear your cry

for you are my all and I want you for the rest of my life

I know you need time and to think about your decision but know I

      am here

I will make a change to gain back your trust

you have access to my heart, please take it from me

look deep down and find all that you want to see

I am here for you, I love you so

please tell me how you feel, I am all yours

time will pass by as we begin our healing process

it will be slow, and painful but I know that our souls are

      meant to be

but for now, we are at rest

you are the light in my life but now only darkness shines

      again

Wildflowers

Let the right kind of love fall into your hands

K.J. Bashford

The minute we are born our cycle of death begins

the clock does not stop

our bodies begin to grow and stretch

forming ourselves into a wild mess

the mind constantly craves more

we want more of what we can't take when we go

getting caught up in the materialistic flow

we forget our roots, the place where we started

from the ground, we are one with the earth

she is our mother, the provider for all

as we die, she collects us

gently making sure our souls find a place to rest

someday we will rise again

To him,

  I haven't found you yet

  I know you are out there way beyond the stars and past the

       moon

maybe someday we will meet

  our souls will cross paths

soon to be intertwined beneath each other's feet

love is a mystery, but I know once I find you it will be solved.

                      Love, her

K.J. Bashford

WEEDS

Wildflowers

You yanked me right out the garden

pulled me all the way from my roots

your hands wrapped around my brittle body so tightly

I was wilted and weak

you deprived me of the things I needed most

the love you gave me was sheltered away from the sunlight

when you got angry, your thorns popped out and you

        thrashed around

my colors bled from my petals as you sliced them open one

        by one

I was so scared

darkness shed over the garden as you continued to grow

I knew I was dying

I was dying because you mistreated me, but I knew once I let

        myself die I could grow again,

 I did what I knew I had to do

I let myself go

each petal fell off of my body

it was slow and gentle process

the earth hugged me softly laying my body down onto the

ground

you watched me as I began to disappear

you thought you had destroyed me

blackness overgrew the garden

for months, it was dead

coldness swept across the stiff air

sorrow seeped through the soil

one day it began to rain

then it poured

the water sunk down into the darkness that you brought

here

the soil overturned

then there was light

the sun beamed down into the garden

the weeds hissed at the burning embers that fell into the

       ground

at last, there I was once again

my tiny self was nestled into the soil

one tiny stem sprouted and I was ready to grow

I knew I would grow stronger and taller

I knew that I could stand up against you

But this time I wasn't alone

I had an entire army of wildflowers that now grew with me

You

you happened again

Wildflowers

Our bodies were entangled together like long wavy vines that

sat beneath the jungle floor

K.J. Bashford

The only time of day you gave me was after hours

Wildflowers

You laugh at me when I tell you I love you

the only conversations I have with you now are with the

thoughts in my head

what happened to us?

seems like everything is a joke

K.J. Bashford

It was going so well

now I don't even know where it's going

Wildflowers

Colors bled from my veins as you sliced me open

your colors did not compliment mine

constant fights back and forth until our canvas looked like a

battle scene

you used me until I was no more, scraped the paint until I

was bone dry

I became brittle and broken

you wanted fresh and new colors

something that you thought would make you happy again

K.J. Bashford

You should never be punished for sharing your feelings

We try so hard in our lives to find that one person we think is
>   perfect for us
when in reality, it is only ourselves who can continue to please our
>   own desires

I was so naive thinking that people would change

You ask me to expose myself to you every other day

next I'm blocked once again

then you go back to her

playing some games,

that shit isn't right

who are you trying to be

you talk to me like I'm less than human

yet we had a whole past together

fuck you

K.J. Bashford

You caused me unnecessary hurt

Wildflowers

I hate what you did to me

you were forceful with your actions

pushing me down, manipulating me

itemizing my body

I tried to run, told you to stop

worse things would happen if I did not listen to you

it was my fault for even running to the monster who unleashed his
     hell onto me

now that it is done I will have to learn to heal and not let these
     demons enter once again

you were a burden to me, to say the least

I will carry my heart as I please

now I can strongly say I am no longer in a battle with myself

time has shown me how to be stronger

I can't change what happened

 it was a mistake

 but I know now that you will never be able to reach me again

K.J. Bashford

You filled my lungs with fire and let them burn

We are not lovers

we are just trouble

K.J. Bashford

The only makeup you wear now is the black circles under

your eyes

Wildflowers

You were everything in my mind

I was nothing in yours

K.J. Bashford

With you, time shattered into a million pieces

Wildflowers

I was just another number in your phone

K.J. Bashford

I hate seeing you so happy

 I don't like the fact that you found her

I want to be happy for you but, it's so hard when you left me

so broken

You were a wasted breath

K.J. Bashford

I beat myself up over the thought of you

Wildflowers

I did not ask for you to open my legs

K.J. Bashford

I let the past come into my future and it fucked

everything up

My emotions grabbed hold of me

they took me by surprise

they led my mind down many different paths

fear told me one thing

but anger shoved him away

then sadness poured tears all over my heart

happiness was the only emotion that stood so far away

K.J. Bashford

You made me swallow your mistakes whole

I digested them as my own

I felt constantly sick as I made excuses for you

my body tried to rid of the illness you caused

constant lies seeped into my veins,

my blood boiled with the mess you created inside of me

but yet this whole time I believed everything was my fault

Wildflowers

My heart is filled by day but as night rolls in,

you come and break it apart

Months of brutal nightmares and restless nights

caught suffocating, drowning or choking while the moon cast

a shadow down on me

you've only worsened the pain

the pain!

my body screams for you, as you attack my mind

I am so tired of this shit

you've put me through so much

after all this time the hurt is still there

waiting and feeding off of my subconscious

it lurks!

I want to pick myself apart

find what is left of you and destroy it

Wildflowers

We touched, but never felt

K.J. Bashford

The heavy bags of sorrow sat under her eyes

Wildflowers

She will seek out the love that she deserves and hopes he

will never achieve

K.J. Bashford

I feel sorry for her

How could you learn to love someone new only weeks after

loving me?

K.J. Bashford

I don't know why you continued to lie to me

when all I ever wanted was the truth from you in the first place

Wildflowers

I still think about you every damn day

K.J. Bashford

I laid down my body onto yours one last time knowing that your

heart had already belonged to her

Wildflowers

I always had to pause my life in order to keep yours

moving

Your love was bound on my body

you branded me with your name

suppressed me into doing or saying things I didn't want to

do

I made so many excuses to defend you

you marked me as property which sometimes became an

inconvenience for you

Wildflowers

You carved at my body until I was inside out of my own skin

K.J. Bashford

I felt less than whole when I was with you

Wildflowers

It is sad knowing that our relationship had an expiration date

printed right on the front

K.J. Bashford

I want all of you

even if it is the last time

Some days it's hard for me to accept that it's over and you

have moved on

K.J. Bashford

I was so naive to let you go in between my legs yet another

time

After you left me,

my feelings for you became even stronger

K.J. Bashford

I was only a pleasurable inconvenience for you

Wildflowers

I unraveled my skin on to yours

I kept you warm

 gave you all of me

 you took that for granted

 it tore me into shreds

K.J. Bashford

The thought of you never fully goes away

Wildflowers

It's just a bad moment

it's not forever

K.J. Bashford

I have let too many unworthy eyes see my body

Because of him, I don't feel worthy of love anymore

K.J. Bashford

He's been coming everywhere with me lately

I can't get him out of my mind

Wildflowers

I've never had sex with you

we only fucked

K.J. Bashford

He said he never wanted to lose me

he went back to her but kept me around

he lost me and then her

now empty hands lay beneath his eyes

but yet we still hold ours out to grab

She is covered in bruises left from the poor soul who decided

to undo himself onto her

markings upon markings

her body lay stiff as he lifted his weight off

she never had time to heal

his words caused her just as much damage as the fingers he

laid upon her did

K.J. Bashford

He was unfaithful to the girl who gave him everything

      a cheater, a liar

someone not to trust, but someone who she trusted to easily

she went back to him, despite knowing it was just lust

no love was ever there

a relationship in disguise

tearing her apart

starting with her fragile beating heart

Wildflowers

The cold air takes my breath away

it sucks in the warmth that is released from my lungs

it's becoming harder to breathe

I can barely swallow

the skin on my lip peels off slowly as I tug on it

my hands are clenched with white knuckles

I'm feeling too anxious

my thoughts begin to pile on

filing into my mind one by one

I feel like I am breaking down

I'm spiraling and spinning out of control

losing my mind on this bumpy ride

water fills beneath my eye lids

as tears drop down my face, I taste the salt on my

      lips

it sinks into my skin

the warm liquid burns my cheeks, scorches my lips

K.J. Bashford

I bite down on my tongue to hold back the sorrow and pain

I know I need help

I'm going to seek it

even if it kills me doing so

LEAVES

K.J. Bashford

Our brittle bodies leaned back against the brick wall of

    the train station

  it was somewhere around 2 a.m. and we had run away

    together

sought-out adventure and thrill

I stood there next to you as you lit up a cigarette

 smoke blew into my face

my eyes were still weary

 you seemed so unsure

what were we really here for anyways?

I look down at my feet, my sneakers were shredded,

    laces bunched up in knots

my pants hung low holding onto my hips

they were soiled with loose threads and rips

the sound of the train filled our ears

we knew it was time

we jumped on the edge

 our journey awaited

Wildflowers

It is only now that you realize you don't deserve me

K.J. Bashford

There is passion in those who really crave it

Wildflowers

She has so much love to give but everyone takes it

away for the wrong reasons

K.J. Bashford

I kept feeding myself to guys who just wanted to take

little bits of me

You had a direct intent to deceive me

K.J. Bashford

Fill the space of emptiness with _____.

We are a copy and paste society

K.J. Bashford

All my emotions come rushing back every time I see you

Wildflowers

I always felt that I had to hide my feelings around you

you didn't seem to care about anyone else's

except your own

K.J. Bashford

Loving you was an understatement

Why am I so stuck on you?

K.J. Bashford

What we had become, went faster than I could say what I

had on my mind

We do not change

only progress

K.J. Bashford

It's funny how people say so many charming things

yet they never seem to mean any of them once the

words leave their mouth

Wildflowers

Lies slithered in and out between her lips

she had to bite her tongue down to stop them

K.J. Bashford

She has fear in her eyes but so much love in her heart

One shot to heart

you weakened my soul

I became fearful of you

you tried to change me into someone that I could never be

you bought me things I didn't like

to please you, I wore things that were too tight

I suddenly caught myself eating mid-bite

"wait" I said to myself I can't eat this or I will be out of

       his sight

flat stomach, tiny waist, big butt is what you wanted

do more of this at the gym or eat less of this is what you

       promoted

puzzled as I was, I started to believe you and looked at

       myself in disgust

I changed for you, I really did

in the end, you still found another flaw

K.J. Bashford

You broke me into a million and one pieces

Wildflowers

Please do yourself a favor

 move on from him

he isn't doing you any favors

Everything is going to be okay

breathe

Be with someone who makes you a priority

K.J. Bashford

I am not over the fact that I lost you, but then I think it's

really you that lost me

Wildflowers

Seems like I can never scrub you off my body

K.J. Bashford

You only found comfort between my legs

You are so unsettling, yet so satisfying

K.J. Bashford

I left everything behind except:

you

The secrets of magic tricks in our relationship were

revealed too soon

K.J. Bashford

You made me feel completely numb

Wildflowers

I think you mixed lust and love together

creating a complicated situation for yourself

K.J. Bashford

You were just a side effect in my life

someone who was meant to be temporary

blurring out my reality from time to time

Wildflowers

Teardrops stained my skin as they rolled down my

cheeks

I wiped them up with the rough of your shirt

my heart, it burned

I gazed into your eyes, looking for comfort

but only loneliness stood in the way

K.J. Bashford

I'll always miss you

Wildflowers

He kept trying to seek the same thing from her that he

once did from me

she was far less the type that he had hoped to encounter

K.J. Bashford

I want to feel happy again

sadness hangs over me

heavy weight sits on my shoulders

I am sinking into the ground

it's crazy to think that I never felt this way until I met you

You don't think you deserve love anymore

he took it all from you

before you even realized what was being done

K.J. Bashford

I held a tiny bottle of pressurized love in my hands

it glistened in the light

small bubbles lined the inside of the glass

it was sealed up tightly, tied with a red ribbon

if I drank it, I'd feel a burst of passion through my heart,

happiness within my lungs

but the love would only be temporary

Your breath tasted like alcohol as you kissed me

you hung heavy over my shoulders

you begged for my body claiming it as yours

 I stared at you with disgust

 a feeling of distrust laid between my legs

a thought occurred to me that I was not the only girl you'd

       sought to please

there were more, at least two or three

I wanted to ignore that thought and put myself at ease

my mind cannot picture it

 my heart does not want to feel the pain that would soon hit

K.J. Bashford

It's been so long, since you've been by my side

the days seem to stretch by as they soon turn into

months

to everyone else it seems so short

to me it feels like an eternity

Wildflowers

My thoughts lay beside me late at night

they speak to me softly and settle in real close

sometimes they are abrupt and uneasy

I stare at them trying to make them disappear

they only creep in closer making it harder to fall asleep

K.J. Bashford

I fell so hard for you

I wanted us to work out so badly

our souls drifted apart

 we were not meant to be

our love felt forced

fire burned in our eyes

we sought pleasure

wanted passion and desire

all we got was a relationship that lacked love instead

Wildflowers

The weeds that grew from her skin was her body's way

of removing the excess damage from her garden

K.J. Bashford

WILDFLOWERS

We must break away from the pain in order to heal

ourselves

K.J. Bashford

A heart will beat for many in a lifetime

but only love those who share the same beat back

Wildflowers

Water droplets dripped slowly down her skin

as she stepped out of the shower

the moonlight peered into the window, glowing upon her

body

in his eyes, she looked like an angel

he held her closely,

wrapping a towel around her followed by his arms

she stole a kiss from him

he smirked and picked her up bringing her into the bedroom

a moment so simple, but so powerful

K.J. Bashford

A burning sensation rushed through my body

everything around me slowed down

chills ran up and down my spine as you pulled me closer

Wildflowers

Know your own damn worth, because he certainly never did

K.J. Bashford

The truth hurts less now because I've known about it all

along

A few months ago, dating was out of the question

not taken to heart or thought out

my soul drifted along, awaiting, for her to be picked

      up again

I carried my heart, hung it over my shoulders

a weight sank down on me

a few months passed by and then it was you I was told I

      would see

there I saw you, so perfect, so sincere

an instant match, a spark, a connection!

funny it is, but I know not to fight these feelings

this is what I want now and for you to be a part of it

let new beginnings bring us together

 we are both special and deserve each other

you showed me kindness and respect

you told me that I can be treated like a queen

you were the lost king I had longed to find

K.J. Bashford

a piece of my heart I give to you

 now we grow together as our journey begins

The summer nights seem to drift by so slowly without you

I gaze upon the moonlight as I hold my heart in my own

   hands

the wind whispers words of hope into my ear

my souls managed to let out a small smile

I want you now but our love cannot be

you and I see things differently

I know we are meant to be

you explained to me that you need time and to take it easy

many months to come ahead as we will reflect on our

   relationship

this space between us will only bring us closer

time will tell as he works his wonder into love

as we wait, we will thrive

we will grow

I love you so

 I hope that one day you will return saying

those gentle words back to me

K.J. Bashford

I know that there is nothing I can say or do to convince you

but just know that I love you

We tend to say things out of frustration if we are in a battle

with ourselves

K.J. Bashford

I miss you every day, but I do not miss the things that you

did to me

Wildflowers

After I left you, I finally started to feel like myself again

K.J. Bashford

Last night was supposed to be fun, until my dress came off

and your pants came undone

Wildflowers

Sometimes we seek out love in the worst ways

K.J. Bashford

My heart tends to dream too big sometimes

You shouldn't feel guilty for loving someone new

When you find the right person, hold them close and never

let go

Wildflowers

We nestled in close to one another, our bodies touched

warmth was the only thing that sat between us

you placed a hand on my cheek and looked at me with

     soft eyes

I stared back and smiled

you pressed your lips into mine, making me want to press

     back harder

I pulled you close

you wrapped your hands around my waist

our lips blended into one, a kiss was planted with so much

     passion

you laid me down onto the bed

we paused to look at each other

I began to undo the lace strings stitched on my top

you didn't take your eyes off of me as you began to

undo the belt on your navy-blue jeans

I lifted up your white cotton t-shirt as your hands slid down

K.J. Bashford

my back

I set my face down on your chest

 your skin was so soft as I ran my hands all over you

 I listened to your heartbeat

you undid the clasp on my bra

you kissed me again

I spread my body down on the mattress

silk sheets covered the bed, casting a glow onto our skin

your body hung over me

I wrapped my legs around your body to let you in

passion poured into the room

love laid its blanket over us

we gasped and moaned with so much emotion

in this moment, our hearts beat as one, minds thinking

on the same wavelength

we found the desire that we had once sought out

elsewhere before

Your kiss left my lips completely numb

K.J. Bashford

The nights stretch by with you on my mind

my thoughts tend to linger

my eyes become glassy against the white moonlight

I shed a tear

not for you, but for myself

the pain I have been through sometimes conquers me again

I'd hope you'd be there for me

not depending on each other but learning to grow together again

where are you now?

please come back to me

I love you so

Water-droplets dripped slowly down her skin

they kissed each part of her so softly

she stepped out of the shower and glanced at the window

the moonlight peaked its way in and poured its light onto her

      body

behind her stood her love

he leaned his body against the wall admiring her and just

      taking all of her beauty in

Tiny snowflakes kissed her lips as they melted from the

      warmth of her body

she leaned her head on his shoulder

they stood together on the sidewalk

his hand held hers as they watched the street lights change

      color

as they pressed their lips together, they melted into one

burning embers sat in the reflection of his eyes

his kiss was so soft that heat between them was like fire

she was so captivated by him

his touch danced across her body making her shiver with

      excitement

in that moment, she felt that their fire would never die

Wildflowers

We posed as one, together forever

we caressed each other

our ears listening close, our minds even closer

we leaned in, saying "I love you" for the very first time

K.J. Bashford

Steam filled the bathroom as we stood in the shower under

the hot water

droplets spread across the green tile

a broken bar of soap slipped on edge

you stood close to me and embraced my body

your hands wrapped around my waist

I pressed into you harder

we kissed slowly, our lips pressing each to each other

you kissed me down my neck, onto my breasts,

I felt the rough of your skin right against mine

something about you makes me feel alive

Wildflowers

I want you to know how strong and amazing you are

if you could see that within yourself, then you know how truly

special you are

you deserve nothing less

K.J. Bashford

You are so empowering that people don't even know what

you are going to unravel

You are only an idea of yourself:

turn that idea into a reality

K.J. Bashford

Be amongst others who are like you

Let all of your colors shine

Bright, dull, shiny, or dark

Your body is painted so beautiful

K.J. Bashford

Sometimes I forget who I am

then out of nowhere

I come running back to myself

in full bloom

Wildflowers

I lacked in being normal, because I knew being out of the

ordinary fit me better

K.J. Bashford

Be yourself

it will take you a lot further than you know

Wildflowers

Her hair flows like a waterfall as she sat back on the

    swing

she swung her legs back and forth flying up into the sky

the wind brushed red onto her cheeks, making her blush

she smiled wide because her beauty was captured in that

    moment

K.J. Bashford

Celebrate you

She caressed herself as she stood in front of the mirror

her towel hung low on her hips, hugging her body

her skin soaked up all the tiny droplets of water that fell from

her hair

she placed her hands on her chest, flexed her arms, and

grabbed her stomach

she tried to picture herself with a different body

but she realized that her true beauty was not from her

physical nature

it was her soul and mind that out did all the rest

K.J. Bashford

I needed a new place to call home

somewhere I could thrive again

a space to stretch my leaves and spread out my petals

as I began my new journey, I stumbled into a new garden

I felt uneasy

my leaves shriveled up and my vibrant colors were washed

out

I did not know if I would fit in here

I am a wildflower

someone who stands high above the weeds, out from behind

the roses

I decided to settle my roots into this new soil

I began to grow here, amongst more wildflowers

I started to like this garden

I bled new colors into my petals as I absorbed the warmth

just as I started to bloom, someone came along and clipped

off my leaves

it stung with pain and I crumbled up, barely holding myself

    together

I wanted to die

then I realized this is where I was supposed to be

I grew once again knowing that sometimes thorns will tear

      you apart but, only to teach you a lesson about life

nobody wanted to hurt me in this garden

everyone here showed me love and support

I embraced each new flower as they became part of my life

my confidence stretched to the sky

the soil beneath me was enriched with new ideas

I knew I was thriving

as the season began to change, I knew I would change

     once again too

after all, that is what wildflowers do

K.J. Bashford

My friends, the love and support you give

I return to you with happiness

you all have so many things to be grateful for

the letters roll in to an acceptance to college

or wedding bells ring as the date approaches,

you are all making connections

growing so far, expanding your life, starting a family

move down the line you are ending relationships but only

to start healthier ones!

you keep moving forward and creating your hearts out

I have no doubt you will all go far

this news brings me joy and tears to my eyes

to see you all thrive makes me wish I didn't have to say

goodbye

you'll always be around the corner or in my back pocket

I will miss you all dearly but know not to fear

for you are my friends, supportive and all here

present you are, how lucky I am

what a joy life is!

the wild experiences it brings us

the wonderment of excitement awaits

open your eyes, life has just begun!

K.J. Bashford

She grew amongst the wildflowers

feeling free and adventurous

she let herself grow

Made in the USA
Middletown, DE
14 October 2021